MULTIVERSE OF HEART

ANURAG TIWARI

Copyright © Anurag Tiwari
All Rights Reserved.

This book has been self-published with all reasonable efforts taken to make the material error-free by the author. No part of this book shall be used, reproduced in any manner whatsoever without written permission from the author, except in the case of brief quotations embodied in critical articles and reviews.

The Author of this book is solely responsible and liable for its content including but not limited to the views, representations, descriptions, statements, information, opinions and references ["Content"]. The Content of this book shall not constitute or be construed or deemed to reflect the opinion or expression of the Publisher or Editor. Neither the Publisher nor Editor endorse or approve the Content of this book or guarantee the reliability, accuracy or completeness of the Content published herein and do not make any representations or warranties of any kind, express or implied, including but not limited to the implied warranties of merchantability, fitness for a particular purpose. The Publisher and Editor shall not be liable whatsoever for any errors, omissions, whether such errors or omissions result from negligence, accident, or any other cause or claims for loss or damages of any kind, including without limitation, indirect or consequential loss or damage arising out of use, inability to use, or about the reliability, accuracy or sufficiency of the information contained in this book.

Made with ♥ on the Notion Press Platform
www.notionpress.com

Contents

Acknowledgements

I would like to express my gratitude to all the people who have been a part of this journey. Everything you will read in this book may have been encountered by you in some form or another. Sometimes you may have been the sufferer, or sometimes the listener to a friend who underwent similar experiences. This book is a collection of those emotions, love, and many hustles that I have tried to put into words. I would like to thank my friends and family for their support and encouragement throughout the writing process. Finally, I would like to thank my readers for taking the time to read this book and for allowing me to share my journey with them.

1. Love's Symphony

Cutleries cutting through cuddles,
Raps rustling through muscles.
The sharp edges slicing the tender meat,
As we feast on the love we cheat.
With each clink of the fork and knife,
Our hearts entwine in bitter strife.
But as the meal comes to an end,
We find our love is not pretend.
For in the rustling of the raps,
We hear the beating of our hearts.
And in the cutting of the cutleries,
We see the strength of our love's varieties.
So let us raise a glass and toast,
To the love that endures and never boasts.
Songs of love fill the air,
As we sit and stare.
Eyes locked in a loving gaze,
Our hearts in a never-ending maze.
The clinking of the cutleries,
Reminds us of love's varieties.
The rustling of the raps,
A symphony of our love's snaps.
As we listen to the songs,
Our hearts begin to hum along.

We sway to the melody,
Our love's a beautiful symphony.
The cutleries, the raps, the songs,
All a part of love's eternal throngs.
As we dine on this feast of love,
We know that our hearts will always be above.
For in this moment, we are one,
Our love, forever, under the sun.
For in this moment, we are whole,
Our love, a story yet to be told.

2. A Walk in the Starry Nights

Lost myself through mirages
Ruptured the depression in naive
Holding beneath my grudges
I walk in those starry nights
With every step, I feel the weight,
Of the mistakes I made and the past I hate.
I see the mirages of who I used to be,
And I realize, it's not who I want to be.
I let go of the grudges I held so tight,
And I start to see the world in a new light.
The stars above, they guide me on my way,
And I find the strength to face another day.
I break free from the depression that held me down,
And I start to see the beauty all around.
I walk in those starry nights,
With a newfound hope, and a heart full of light.
I find my way, through the dark and the fear,
And I realize, my future is so very dear.
With each step, I leave the past behind,
And I embrace the journey of life, with an open mind.
With a new perspective and a will to live,
I realize, the best is yet to give.

3. Echoes of Love

That song you played, it brings me back
To the days when we first met.
Naive me, I fell for your melody,
And the memories of you, they still linger in me.
Memories of the one whom I loved and cherished,
The one who made my heart flutter and my soul perish.
We were young and in love, nothing could tear us apart,
We were each other's world, a work of art.
We laughed, we cried, we shared our dreams,
We whispered sweet nothings, under the moon's beams.
We walked hand in hand, under the starry skies,
We whispered I love you's, as we closed our eyes.
But little did I know, that love would soon fade,
As I lost myself in the chaos that I made.
I let my ego, my pride get in the way,
I let my mistakes, ruin what we had that day.
And before I knew it, it was too late,
I had lost the love, that was once so great.
And now, that song you played, it brings me back,
To the moments we shared, and the memories we had.
Those memories of the one I loved and cherished,
Are now lost in an apocalypse of my own deeds.
I miss those nights, filled with love, complaints and rains,
Rains that you loved so much, I still see us in dreams.

Holding hands, and walking under the moon,
Posing for a click, and a peek to the past.
I wish I could turn back time,
And relive those moments that didn't last.
But all I have now, is this song you played,
A reminder of the love we shared, and the price I paid.
It echoes through my heart, and my mind,
A haunting melody, of a love that was once mine.
And so I listen, to that song you played,
As I close my eyes, and let the memories invade.
I'll hold on to them, and never let them go,
For the love we shared, is something I'll always know.
Even though it's gone, and we've moved on,
That song you played, will always live on.
As a reminder, of the love we shared,
And the memories, that will always be there.

4. The Ghosts of My Mind

The ghosts that I live with, they never leave my side,
They haunt my life with blood and make my heart hide.
I put on a brave face, and I smile in your smile,
I clap to cheer you, but inside, I'm dying all the while.
Back in my cave, I live with these monsters,
Monsters that seek pain, and curse for me.
They lurk in the shadows, and feed on my fears,
They make me feel like a prisoner of my own tears.
I've lived a million cursed lives, and breached every hack,
But still the pain within me, it refuses to hack.
I try to run, but they follow me still,
These ghosts that I live with, they haunt me still.
I try to fight them, but they're too strong,
They make me feel like I'll never belong.
They tear me apart, piece by piece,
Until I'm nothing but a shell, a release.
I try to find solace, in the darkness of night,
But the monsters come alive, and give me a real fight.
I try to scream, but no sound comes out,
My voice is lost, in this endless bout.
I'm trapped in this cycle, of pain and despair,
I'm dying every moment, without a care.
I'm lost in this abyss, with no way out,
I'm a prisoner, of my own doubt.

I try to hold on, to the hope of light,
But it's getting harder, to fight this fight.
I'm slipping away, into the void,
Leaving behind, all that I've enjoyed.
The ghosts that I live with, they've won in the end,
I'm dying, without a friend.

5. The Last Embrace

Maybe this night will be my last, with pain my only companion,
But tomorrow awaits, with newer hopes and loves from you.
With every moment passing by, I cherish these few days,
Fewer days of your skin I touched and the smell I nibbled.
Those arms that wrapped me and the chest so passionate,
The memories of you, they'll forever last.
I'll hold on to them, as I take my last breath,
For in your love, I found my final death.
I remember the first time I saw you,
My heart skipped a beat, and I knew it was true.
You were the one, the love of my life,
The one that made everything feel right.
We laughed, we cried, we loved,
We shared our hopes, our dreams and our troubles.
With every kiss, every touch, every look,
I knew that my love for you would never be mistook.
But now as I lay here, on my deathbed,
I can't help but think, of all the things we said.
The promises we made, the love we swore,
Will never come true, that's what I'm scared for.
But even in death, I'll never let you go,
For the love we shared, it was too strong to know.
I'll hold on to you, till the very end,
And hope that in the next life, we'll love again.

So as I close my eyes, and say my final goodbyes,
I'll hold on to the memories of you, and the love we shared, until I die.
I'll hold on to the hope that one day, we'll meet again,
And our love will be stronger, than it ever was back then.

6. Lover Caveman

I, the random guy, who is a caveman now,
Writes to you with all the agonies I behold.
The nights on the couch were soothing,
But now they're filled with emptiness and cold.
The gifts you gave me, they still smell like you,
A reminder of the love we once knew.
I feel those painful puns you smiled at me,
Though unexpressed, they still dent my heart with glee.
Through the winter cravings, I behold,
The memories of you, they never grow old.
I've learnt those sarcastic aromas of yours,
The essence of jasmine, forever yours.
A thousand kilometers away,
You still linger in my thoughts every day.
I imagine you, under those concrete walls,
Stabbing your emotions, every night as you fall.
Though we're apart, you're still with me,
In every smile, in every memory.
I still miss you, my love, my life,
I'll always crave for you, through every strife.
I miss the way your hair falls on your face,
I miss the way your lips taste.
I miss the way you look at me,
With those eyes that make me feel so free.

I miss the way you touch me,
The way you make me feel complete.
I miss the way you hold me,
And make me feel like nothing can ever control me.
I miss thesound of your voice,
The way it makes me rejoice.
I miss the way you move,
The way you make me groove.
I miss the way you laugh,
The way it makes my heart dance.
I miss the way you moan,
The way it makes my body groan.
I miss the way we make love,
The way our bodies fit like a glove.
I miss the way we explore,
The way our passion is something we can't ignore.
I miss you, my love, my life,
I'll always crave for you, through every strife.
I'll wait for the day, when we'll be together,
And our love will last forever.

7. If

If ever they asked how far did, I go?
Tell them I went far, quite far.
Away from the sways and ways of life
Away from those bewildering lies.
I took a step one sunny noon
And I do cry under every moon.
Yes, I do miss the ones whom I left and lost,
But, no one grasped me when I needed it
If ever they asked, why did I go?
Tell them I was quivered with life
The quantum and realms were all a lie.
I asked the sun before I leapt out from this Universe,
Un due like others, he told me about the multiverse.
I got lost on an unending voyage,
Where my life was not mine.
Beholding no emotions and pains
(As what the world wanted)
I started my journey that sunny noon in my tide.
I lost count of time at various tides,
I lost my family and my faith in those splashing waves.
I kept learning my formulas tried to dwell them in a universe,
A universe which hold a substitute of me in some other verse.
Yet I kept travelling, weeping at the corridors of life and time
I lost my patience and the human I used to be.

This hackamore created a null chamber.
And I sit here reading, writing, and listening to my own words.
Words which hold no means now.
Now as in this universe coz'
Maybe in some other they must be wetting your eyes enough.
This journey gave me something special,
Things I can't behold,
Things I can't cherish,
Things I can't think anymore,
Things that no longer will be things.
Everything will be just a multistring paranoid
A paranoid of my thoughts, hunger, and an unending zeal.
So, here I am closing this poem in this verse.
With ecstasy for you and also for me
Me who is still listening, reading, and feeling these countless words
In some long far away verse!

8. The Sun and its Allies

Its awaited and I am writing this,
I asked her for moonly thoughts, she burned me with sunny words.
Its a roast yes coz' I love her, and she said She loves my hobbies.
So back in Corona summer we adored and right now we glow.
Broked her somewhere in between but now glowing adorably.
She is the SUn and her thoughts for me are her allies.
I am writing it straight coz she is witty but fails in my poems always,
The audience has always adored my metaphors and this lady hops no good to my words.
Complains and witts are always bombing on me.
Caricature of my half dull full down life
this woman is Sun of my life.
Somewhere in mid-Autumn hit, thats what I feel.
Somewhere in mid Chill barca loses, this lady is that half dead audience.
She loves me with her wit but cant afford mine.
What an irony of life!
A roaster being unroasted here.
I gave her the header fo these lines but yet she couldnt define,
Love, audacity and a little grilling, this is everyday story.
With all my joy she kicks me out of her room and with all hues, she hugs me tight!
I love you I said in her native tongue and she couldn't teach me a sentence from then.

Its an awaited promise yet, though she is Sun of my life and her thoughts are the allies.
Wish she could know how much she means to me.
I am the wolf to this Sun and the absorber of her Allies.
When evrything goes normal she hits back to my failures.
haha! its interesting yet its a challenge.
This glassgow is yet to be written more
with coming time the words will grow and so will my love
The Sun and allies is a grill of love and emotions and the lost Metaphors

9. Blank Space

A space so solace its all tied with lace,
Lace of fear, anguish, trauma, loss.
Every council you dictate, every principal you narrate,
No worth no crap. Shits do happen man!
Some tendencies are unreal, some totally irony.
I couldnt hug and say how much I wanted,
I couldnt bestow my inner peace with her
Unreal sarcastic the realm has turned up
Worthless have become these poems.
When the queen of elegancy aint there,
Whats the joint for a poem?
To every loss of 7 years to every pain of 7 months
Lets sabotage things.
You aint know my pain and yeah So do I
Accepting my part,
This blank space itches hard.
It cripples every yarn, every notion,
You curse, you rush.
You heal the things, for which you are always right.
Unready and all arrogant for my part,
The fear of blank space is more grilling than those curses.
Stand in a row of unpredicted paths and stand in a dark forest,
Melody is always on paths not on dead surrows,
Blank space is a timid lace of time.

You stand out somewhere in dark
Still waiting for them to hold you back.
A mere touch in the blank space is must
I wish for you!
Just a hold and every dearth will vanish.
Blank space is a paranoid, a hill of shadows
No eyes, no face
Only fear and a rear escape you look for.
A lively person can have an escape,
A psychopath will be crunched to egoistic downfalls,
Merely ending up in blank space
Every minute grain can be build
If you hold me tight
To eternity, I stand for you.

10. No Poems for Her

Yes, you complain and yes, I don't write for you.
My words don't have that ecstasy,
The words who a looted every emotion and notion
Now, don't stand a chance to make you feel good about me.
Yes, I am the ruler and I am the game were my words
And they always will be.
But my lady, they don't utter any chance of whispering in front of you.
I am a sack of billion armours who can break any obscene
When it comes to hold you in my scene,
My words they just run away.
Typically I have found we gallop like thousand chirps
We belong to the same agony, aspects and vents.
You hold the misogyny of me
While I behold your shadow every fucking time.
Haha, words though do hurt and rest though cant fulfil.
You are the persona of me
I am your lullaby.
Grasp the thoughts which I have for you
My lady I don't write for you
Coz' these useless words are worthless until the day
We sink in together forever and ever.
I swear we will vibe for a billion notes,
We will scribble a zillion thoughts
On the sands of time, I will hold you in my arms

My back on all worldly mentos
My eyes all on you.
My lady my girl
I will hold you till my last breath.
A night of surveillances and pain
can't justify my love for you.
A billion actions of blind pushes in me are running every now and then.
I hold up my tears all for you and only for you.
Not just being your Man, But being your Maan.
Zillion agonies I have
little I cry, I touch and fall for you every time I thrive.
With this I close my worthless words expressing my
Priceless thoughts for you!

9 798889 518693

Printed by Libri Plureos GmbH in Hamburg,
Germany